W9-BGX-070

Skilled Jobs in
ENGINEERING

Pat Rarus

ReferencePoint
Press®

San Diego, CA

About the Author

Pat Rarus loves writing, especially about technology. She holds a bachelor of arts degree in journalism and a master of science degree in mass communications, both from San Diego State University. She has worked as a professional writer and editor for more than twenty years and lives in Oceanside, California.

For more information, contact:
ReferencePoint Press, Inc.
PO Box 27779
San Diego, CA 92198
www.ReferencePointPress.com

Picture Credits:

Cover: GaudiLab/Shutterstock
10: goodluz/Shutterstock.com
19: RGStudio/Shutterstock.com
40: sturti/Shutterstock.com
49: GCShutter/Shutterstock.com
56: Gorodenkoff/Shutterstock.com
65: Kinwun/Shutterstock.com

LIBRARY OF CONGRESS CATALOGING-IN-PUBLICATION DATA

Names: Rarus, Pat, author.
Title: Skilled jobs in engineering / by Pat Rarus.
Description: San Diego, CA : ReferencePoint Press, Inc., 2021. | Series: Jobs for skilled workers | Includes bibliographical references and index.
Identifiers: LCCN 2019053950 (print) | LCCN 2019053951 (ebook) | ISBN 9781682828212 (library binding) | ISBN 9781682828229 (ebook)
Subjects: LCSH: Engineering--Vocational guidance--Juvenile literature.
Classification: LCC TA157 .R34 2021 (print) | LCC TA157 (ebook) | DDC 620.0023--dc23
LC record available at https://lccn.loc.gov/2019053950
LC ebook record available at https://lccn.loc.gov/2019053951

Contents

Great Careers at Half the Cost and Time

In 2019 an FBI probe found that wealthy parents paid between $250,000 and $450,000 per student, and some as much as $6.5 million, to Rick Singer, founder and chief executive officer of college consulting firm the Key, to illegally boost their children's SAT scores so their kids could get into elite universities such as Yale, Georgetown, Stanford, and the University of Southern California. This massive scandal dominated news headlines for months and incriminated high-profile celebrities. Among the guilty were Oscar-nominated actress Felicity Huffman, who had to serve a two-week prison sentence, pay a $30,000 fine, and perform 250 hours of community service.

While a four-year bachelor's degree from a prestigious university may be a big deal to the rich and famous, thousands of other families have discovered a far less expensive yet highly successful alternative: a two-year associate's degree from a community or technical college. In fact, as far back as 2002, the Bureau of Labor Statistics (BLS) published a special report touting the merits of such a degree, especially one involving engineering or technology. Two well-paying and in-demand jobs—aerospace engineering technician (with a median salary of $67,010), and robotics technician, ($57,790)—are listed in the BLS report and profiled in this book.

New Opportunities as Older Workers Retire

As technology becomes more sophisticated and baby boomers (those born from 1946 to 1964) retire and leave the workforce, many technology jobs need to be filled. Tiffni Deeb, chief information officer for Minneapolis Community and Technical College, explains that in her state, there are "many large corporations with over a thousand technology jobs open now because [applicants] don't have the skills. . . . That [associate's] degree is going to continue to be meaningful in our world."[1]

Other educators as well as human resources managers—those who hire new employees—agree that there is a pressing need for workers who can troubleshoot and then repair high-tech devices. This could, for example, include figuring out the cause of a mechanical or electrical defect in an airplane part or a malfunction in a robot on the factory floor that helps assemble vehicles. Most teens already know a lot about electronics because using cell phones and other portable gadgets are a big part of their lives. With this ability, they just need to develop their technology talents for specific projects and uses. "Individuals who can navigate electronic games, are good with technology, and possess the ability to reason mechanically are perfect candidates for aviation technology and maintenance," says Chris A. Pipesh, vice president of education for MIAT College of Technology in Canton, Michigan. "Aviation has numerous opportunities in defense, manufacturing, aerospace, the airline industry and many others."[2]

Tech Prospects Are Improving for Females

In addition to a shortage of skilled technology workers, many engineering jobs go unfilled because girls and young women have traditionally been discouraged from pursuing careers in science, technology, engineering, and math (STEM). Fortunately, that mindset is changing. In the aerospace sector, for example, large manufacturing companies are offering scholarships and other educational funding opportunities to women. In 2018 Boeing and the Boeing Company Charitable Trust partnered with more than 140 STEM organizations and contributed more than $19 million toward community initiatives that helped inspire an estimated 630,000 young women to pursue a STEM-related career, according to a 2019 post on Boeing's website. Smaller but still important scholarships are available from a wide variety of organizations, such as Women in Aviation International, which offered $948,500 in funds in 2019.

After aspiring female engineering technicians obtain their training, they may be faced with other challenges once on the job, such as being accepted by their male coworkers. "You need a bit of backbone if you're going to put up with the boys; luckily, I grew up with two brothers that prepared me for this my whole life," airframe and power plant mechanic Casey Wutzke explains. "You have to keep your eye on the prize, that's for sure . . . but I must say, everyone I have ever met in this industry is absolutely amazing. I wouldn't want to be anywhere else!"[3]

Rewarding Work

Although money, health care benefits, flexible schedules, and opportunities for advancement are important to today's engineering technology workers, helping others also ranks high on the list. "OH&S (occupational health and safety) is a noble profession, one where you can really help people," says safety consultant and former global construction safety and risk manager Don Schmid. "Your work can help to make sure that a mom, dad, son or daughter returns home safely to their family."[4] Schmid's decades-long career in health and safety for the Ford Motor Company shows that working in a field that fulfills one's passion while helping others may be the greatest reward of all. Fortunately, skilled jobs in engineering offer many such opportunities.

Environmental Engineering Technician

What Does an Environmental Engineering Technician Do?

Teens who are interested in protecting the planet's natural resources may have a strong inclination toward this important work. Environmental engineering is concerned with safeguarding people from adverse ecological effects, such as pollution, as well as improving environmental quality.

Today pollution is a reality that humans have to deal with. Major sources of it are trash, car emissions, and industrial waste. Fortunately, people can all breathe a little easier with environmental engineering technicians (EETs) on the job. These dedicated professionals test the water, air, and soil to help find ways to lessen the impact of pollution. In addition, they work to improve recycling, waste disposal, and public health, as well as control water and air pollution. "I find environmental engineering to be an exciting field because you can actually develop and build solutions to environmental problems,"[5] says Clifford Goertemiller, who works in the Office for Sustainability at Harvard University.

EETs carry out the plans that environmental engineers develop. They test, operate, and if necessary, modify equipment used to prevent or clean up environmental pollution. They may collect samples for testing or work to lessen sources of environmental pollution. They also order materials from vendors to keep laboratories adequately supplied with critical equipment. In addition, they arrange to dispose of hazardous materials such as asbestos and lead, and they inspect facilities to assure that laws and regulations are properly observed.

Depending on the organization's focus, an EET who works for an oil company might find him- or herself setting up experiments to test new methods for cleaning up oil spills. Another task may be to test water downstream from a factory to determine whether pollution control requirements are being met. Yet another duty may involve inspecting and maintaining the machinery in a recycling plant. EETs who work in hospitals take care of properly handling and disposing of biological waste. Disposing of medical waste and garbage requires following special procedures, since bodily fluids are regarded as biohazards. "Given the number of germs in a medical facility, an environmental service position is the front line employee, ensuring a safe environment for patients, visitors and medical personnel,"[6] says career counselor Kelly S. Meier, who advises students at Minnesota State University, Mankato.

A Typical Workday

An EET's day is filled with variety—a combination of indoor and outdoor activities—which keeps him or her hopping from one task to another with little chance of getting bored. The day usually starts by reviewing work plans to schedule activities, as well as answering emails from supervisors and team members. These may include scientists, engineers, and technicians who work where the EET does—at a government agency such as a water district or at a consulting firm that does business with a government agency.

While in the field, the EET may collect samples of air, soil, water, and other materials for laboratory analysis. After collection, he or

Lighting Up a Hospital Room

"As the Environmental Services lead [technician] I enjoy most performing a fluorescent test to ensure that my employees are [disposing of waste] and cleaning hospital patients' rooms thoroughly. The white fluorescent powder that I use lights up if the aide missed cleaning a key part of the hospital room such as the toilet handle. Depending on how the aide did, we would possibly have to perform the test again either the same day or within the week to ensure the aide improved in this area."

—Eric Padilla, environmental services lead technician at Tri-City Medical Center in Oceanside, California

Eric Padilla, email interview with the author, September 22, 2019.

she needs to clearly label, track, and ensure the purity of the samples being transported to the laboratory. Once back at the lab, the EET uses equipment such as a microscope to evaluate and analyze the samples to see whether there are any pollutants or other toxins.

After analyzing the samples, the EET prepares charts and reports that summarize test results. He or she then discusses test results and analyses with the supervisor, who then presents these findings to the client (if the EET works for a consulting firm) or to a committee (if the EET works for a government agency). "Beginning environmental technicians work under the direct supervision of an environmental scientist or a more senior technician," explains career development facilitator Dawn Rosenberg McKay. "With experience, they'll receive only general supervision and can eventually supervise those with less experience."[7]

Environmental scientists, who typically have at least a bachelor of science degree, usually have management responsibilities. Depending on where they work, their duties may include working with businesses, governments, and the general public on health risks and environmental hazards. Once they do this, they choose the best data collection method for research projects. The workers they supervise—EETs—then collect this data. EETs who are

on the job for a few years may be promoted to a senior EET position. In addition to a higher salary, they also get more responsibilities. For example, they may help their environmental scientist manager prepare reports and give presentations to their organization's senior-level executives.

Education and Training

EETs typically need an associate's degree in environmental science, environmental health, public health, or a related degree. In high school, students should take courses in chemistry, biology, math, and physics. Course work in statistics and computer science is also useful. Laboratory experience is helpful as well, and students can get this through their high school or community college science courses. In addition, since EETs may write reports for their supervisors, students may wish to enroll in a journalism class or work on their school newspaper, website, or yearbook.

When their school day is over, budding EETs can get hands-on experience by joining environmental organizations such as the Sierra Club and/or volunteering for community service projects related to the environment. College students can work as summer interns in programs sponsored by various agencies and groups, including the US Environmental Protection Agency, the National Park Service, and the National Science Foundation. This type of experience enables students to develop practical environmental and research skills and enhances one's résumé.

Skills and Personality

EETs need to be problem solvers in order to sort out data and test results, draw logical conclusions, and recommend effective solutions for environmental problems. "You will like this career if you are someone who likes work activities that include practical, hands-on problems and solutions," according to the career site OwlGuru. "[EETs] like working with plants, animals, and real-world materials like wood, tools, and machinery. [They] also like working with ideas, and require an extensive amount of thinking. They like searching for facts and figuring out problems mentally."[8]

In addition to these analytical skills, physical fitness is essential as well. EETs often need to walk long distances and even hike and climb through rough terrain. This requires energy and endurance. Sometimes lifting and moving heavy equipment may also be a part of the job. For that reason, muscular strength makes a big difference.

Working Conditions

EETs typically work full time, both indoors in an office and/or lab and outdoors in the field. Working in the field exposes them to all types of weather. While performing fieldwork, EETs should be able to remain standing or crouching for long periods. They may also be exposed to toxic materials, so they must be trained and knowledgeable in safety measures. In addition, they may need to travel with their supervisors to meet with clients or to perform fieldwork, either of which may require them to work additional or irregular hours.

While EETs usually command the respect of their coworkers, sometimes they may be viewed suspiciously by them. Why? Well, some employees may think that an EET could report them for doing something wrong. For example, they could be putting hazardous material in a regular container, says Joe Proulx, an applied engineering technology instructor at Northcentral Technical College in Wausau, Wisconsin. That is something EETs would need to report and correct, which can sometimes make them unpopular among the people they are monitoring. Still, Proulx explains that the job's benefits to society far outweigh any possibly negative feelings from coworkers. "You're doing the right thing to protect the environment—that in itself can be a great reward," says Proulx. "If you're able to come up with a plan or make an improvement [to the environment], it's rewarding to know what you're doing for the local community."[9]

Employers and Pay

Many EETs work for local, state, or federal agencies or scientific consulting firms that offer environmental services to businesses and other organizations. Other EETs are employed by social advocacy organizations, hospitals, architectural and engineering companies, and the gas and petroleum industry.

EET salaries vary considerably relative to what region they are working in, what industry they serve, and how much experience they have. Other factors that will influence their pay include what company they work for and whether they are in a contract or permanent position. The most highly compensated EETs work for the government, with a median annual salary of $50,560, or $24.31 per hour, according to a 2018 report from the Bureau of Labor Statistics (BLS). The top 10 percent earn an annual salary of more than $82,800, or $39.81 per hour. The bottom 10 percent earn less than $32,380, or $15.57 an hour.

Making the World a Better Place

"Being an environmental engineering technician is a fulfilling career. I get to spend most of my days outside at job sites which I really enjoy. Driving from site to site gives a real sense of freedom with the work I'm doing. I'm responsible for many different tasks including monitoring and collecting samples from vapor extraction systems, assisting with groundwater and vapor probe monitoring, and the occasional day in the office helping with data entry on reports. Having a variety of duties keeps work fresh and exciting. I'm proud that the work I'm involved in is making the world a cleaner, healthier place."

—Megan Fero, environmental engineering technician at Fero Environmental Engineering in Brea, California

Megan Fero, email interview with the author, September 24, 2019.

What Is the Future Outlook for Environmental Engineering Technicians?

The BLS reports that employment for EETs is expected to grow by 9 percent through 2028, which is a little more than average. The jobs will be in demand for these reasons: heightened awareness about the environment, shifting environmental laws and regulations, and the increasing need by businesses to help minimize the effect their operations have on the environment. With those factors in mind, students who decide to become EETs should be able to find fulfilling careers that empower them to change the world for the better.

Find Out More

California Department of Fish and Wildlife
website: www.wildlife.ca.gov

The California Department of Fish and Wildlife helps prevent and rectify environmental problems in the state. The website of this government agency offers EETs educational videos, interviews with environmental scientists, and useful information about environmental issues and volunteer opportunities.

EnvironmentalScience.org
website: www.environmentalscience.org

This website promotes environmental science as a field of study. It offers useful information for EETs about environmental science degree programs, scholarships, internships, careers in different environmental specialties, and job postings.

National Institute of Environmental Health Sciences (NIEHS)
website: www.niehs.nih.gov

The NIEHS is part of the National Institutes of Health. Its mission is to investigate how environmental factors affect human health. It offers a wealth of information about environmental issues, a summer internship program for high school students, and news articles, among other information.

US Environmental Protection Agency (EPA)
website: www.epa.gov

The EPA is a government agency dedicated to protecting the environment. Its website offers lots of information about all kinds of environmental topics, paid and unpaid internships, and job postings; environmental news; a blog; and interviews with environmental scientists.

Aerospace Engineering and Operations Technician

A Few Facts

Number of Jobs
About 10,500 as of 2018

Pay
About $67,010 per year, or $32.22 per hour

Educational Requirements
Associate's degree in engineering technology, computer programming, or robotics machining

Personal Qualities
Math, communication, interpersonal, and critical-thinking skills; mechanical mindset, attention to detail

Work Settings
Indoors in manufacturing or industrial plants, laboratories, and offices

Future Job Outlook
Growth of 7 percent through 2028

What Does an Aerospace Engineering and Operations Technician Do?

Anyone who has ever been afraid to fly in an airplane can be thankful for the work of aerospace engineering and operations technicians (AEOTs). It is their duty to make sure that airplanes are up to snuff by repairing defects and performing scheduled maintenance. More and more, these tech-savvy employees are using computer-based modeling and simulation tools and processes on the job, as well as advanced automation and robotics. Their work is critical for preventing the failure of key parts of new airplanes, spacecraft, and missiles.

Now is a good time to pursue this career because there is a growing need for safe aircraft. "The technological sophistication of airplanes will increase as a modern fleet of airplanes begins to replace outdated aircraft," states the Michigan Institute of Aviation and Technology (MIAT). "There will be an expansion in the aviation market with an increase in income spent on air travel, new routes, and an increase in the number of first-time flyers."[10]

One Woman's Path to a Hands-on Career

"I was [a] sophomore in high school, and I heard through my counselor that they were going to start a program in manufacturing. I took it and found out that I really liked it because I enjoyed working with my hands. Then I went on to Manchester Community College. I started out in architecture and then in my second semester I switched to the aerospace technician courses because I remembered how much I liked the hands-on work in my high school manufacturing class. I was lucky to get an internship at Pratt & Whitney and that led to a fulltime job."

—Elizabeth Comacho, aerospace technician at Pratt & Whitney

Quoted in Revolvy, "A Day in the Life of an Aerospace Technician," June 2017. www.revolvy.com.

AEOTs build test facilities and then run simulations on prototypes or new models to find problems in aircraft design or function. They also record test data and make adjustments to prevent dangerous equipment failures. "Making live tests function as intended requires both communication skills and technical skills," reports the career website Your Free Career Test. "Often when something isn't working, technicians and engineers troubleshoot together, so technicians must know how to ask the questions that will lead to the right answers."[11]

A Typical Workday

An AEOT's workday usually begins by meeting with his or her supervisor—likely an aerospace engineer—and finding out what specific tests need to be conducted that day. New aircraft designs undergo years of testing before they are put into service, because the failure of key parts during flight can be fatal. For that reason a wide variety of tests are performed every day.

As part of their workday, technicians may program and run computer simulations that test new designs. They often must calibrate or measure test equipment such as wind tunnels and determine causes of equipment malfunctions. A wind tunnel is a long tube enclosed in glass, plastic, metal, or sometimes an entire building. Wind tunnels have a high-powered fan on both ends of the tube. Models of aircraft or actual aircraft can be mounted in a wind tunnel so that flight conditions can be simulated, or mimicked, and engineers can study how well a design will fly.

Royce Wagner is an aerospace engineering technician at GE Aviation's Leading Edge Aviation Propulsion engine manufacturing and repair facility in Lafayette, Indiana. Wagner describes his position as being multifaceted. "You have to be technically proficient with your skills and hands, and also cognitively proficient, able to troubleshoot items and understand what can make them go wrong,"[12] he says. After testing various parts of the airplane (its components, assemblies, and mechanisms) to make sure it is safe and working properly, AEOTs record and interpret the data. If they detect major problems with any part of the plane's components, they let their supervisor know immediately and document the information in their written report.

Education and Training

Students can prepare for AEOT training while still in high school by taking classes in advanced math, sciences, and drafting. These classes will give them a head start for the course work they will take at a vocational school or community college. Drafting involves creating plans and blueprints on a computer based on designs for aircraft and related parts. Technology writer Elvis Michael recommends that students pursue an educational program approved by the Accreditation Board for Engineering and Technology (ABET). Most such programs result in an associate's degree in aerospace engineering technology. Michael also recommends that students obtain an internship or cooperative program if such opportunities are available in their area. "These programs often lead to full-time employment after graduating with an associate's degree," he says. "An internship or cooperative program allows students to gain hands-on experience working with aerospace equipment."[13]

After studying for two years, students typically take a written test as well as a practical one. The practical test is a hands-on demonstration in which students can showcase their knowledge of aircraft equipment. Once students pass both tests, they receive their airframe and power plant license, which is regulated by the Federal Aviation Administration (FAA). In addition to licensing, some AEOTs need a government security clearance to work on projects related to national defense.

Skills and Personality

To succeed in the demanding yet rewarding field of aerospace engineering, aspiring AEOTs need a combination of high-tech and people-oriented skills. The high-tech part involves strong math and mechanical skills. They use the principles of mathematics for measurement, analysis, design, and troubleshooting tasks in their work. In addition, AEOTs need mechanical skills to correctly and safely move aircraft parts from design into production.

Their people skills should include a strong ability to communicate because AEOTs talk often with their aerospace engineer supervisors, who give them detailed instructions about testing equipment and other safety issues. AEOTs must be able to understand and follow those instructions, as well as explain any problems to their supervisors. In addition, they need critical-thinking skills. "Aerospace engineering and operations technicians must be able to help aerospace engineers troubleshoot particular design issues," states the Bureau of Labor Statistics (BLS). "[They] must also be able to help evaluate system capabilities, identify problems, formulate the right question, and then find the right answer."[14]

Perhaps most important of all, AEOTs need a passion for airplanes—curiosity about what makes them run and excitement about riding in one, even if they are not licensed pilots. Casey Wutzke, age twenty-seven, grew up in rural Michigan with a grandfather who had a pilot's license and built model airplanes

in his spare time. In 2017 she and her grandfather, uncle, and mother took a fifteen-minute flight in a vintage 1929 New Standard open cockpit biplane, an experience that changed her life. "The scent, the scenery, and the feeling of freedom made me feel that, for a minute, I was the only one up there," Wutzke recalls. "In that moment, I knew I had found my calling."[15]

In November 2017 Wutzke began her two-year aviation education at MIAT in Canton, Michigan. One year later, she obtained an aviation assistant position with a Fortune 500 firm that owns and operates its corporate aircraft. In October 2019 she officially became an airframe and power plant mechanic after passing nine FAA-regulated exams to obtain her mechanic's license.

Testing Airplane Seats for Safety

"We see every product line from super-first class to economy class. With that kind of variety we're really able to get a hands-on feel for the product itself. I work on product certification testing and development on our interior systems seating. We're testing to meet an injury criteria threshold that allows us to constitute it a pass or a fail. It's very short, very fast. The test is happening under these conditions, which is worst-case scenario in the aircraft. It's nice to work with your teammates every day and all have a collective goal, and to accomplish that goal; it's a good feeling."

—Nick Whaley, aerospace engineering technician at Collins Aerospace in Winston-Salem, North Carolina

Quoted in Collins Aerospace, "A Day in the Life of an Engineering Technician," YouTube, May 16, 2019. www.youtube.com/watch?v=aHylo7PO4WY.

Working Conditions

AEOTs usually work in manufacturing or industrial plants, laboratories, and offices. Some of these workers may be exposed to hazards from equipment or toxic materials, but accidents are rare as long as proper procedures are followed. When beginning AEOTs start working on aircraft, they are observed carefully by experienced engineers, mechanics, and inspectors to make sure that their work is performed safely and accurately.

Employers and Pay

AEOTs are employed throughout the private sector with large manufacturing organizations such as Boeing, Northrop Grumman, Lockheed Martin, Airbus, Raytheon, BAE Systems, SpaceX, Rolls-Royce, Pratt & Whitney, and Collins Aerospace, as well as smaller manufacturing companies nationwide. The military also employs AEOTs, particularly the air force, navy and army. Most AEOTs who work for the government are actually contractors who are technically employed by private companies but work on military projects.

The median salary for AEOTs is $67,010 per year, or $32.22 per hour, according to a 2018 report from the BLS. However, government statistics fall short of telling the real story. "I believe their data is lagging [behind] the current trend," says Chris A. Pipesh, vice president of education for MIAT College of Technology. "Wages and benefits are increasing at a rate I haven't seen in my 40-plus years in this industry. . . . Earning a six-figure salary [$100,000 or more a year] is much more attainable than it was just five years ago."[16]

What Is the Future Outlook for AEOTs?

Employment of AEOTs is projected to grow by 7 percent through 2028, about as much as the average for all professions, according to the BLS, with about 120,000 more AEOTs needed by 2028. However, the government data on this topic might actually be too conservative. Employment statistics may not address how many older workers are retiring from the aviation industry. With airplanes becoming increasingly dependent on computer software to operate safely, technicians entering the field must know the latest ways to program the equipment and update it regularly. Failure to do so could result in the loss of human life. For this reason, airplane manufacturers are aggressively seeking workers with these skills. "All segments of the aviation industry are facing detrimental shortages with regard to skilled technicians," says Pipesh, who uses a career fair his school held as an example of prospective growth. "We had over 60 employers, representing various fields and industries, including aviation, trying to recruit students and graduates to fill the gaps in their respective industries."[17] With rising salaries and the satisfaction of keeping air travelers safe, this can be an immensely rewarding job.

Find Out More

Aerospace and Electronic Systems Society (AESS)
website: http://ieee-aess.org

This high-profile aerospace and electronics organization has a mission to introduce careers in technology to students around the world. Students and young professionals are featured widely in the AESS quarterly email blast. Students are also invited to attend the annual Radar Summer School, a two-day conference that offers cutting-edge information about radar technology.

American Institute of Aeronautics and Astronautics (AIAA)
website: www.aiaa.org

The AIAA is a professional aerospace organization providing year-round events, courses, workshops, and online learning opportunities. The AIAA has an online career center for both employers and job seekers. AIAA members have growth opportunities as well as access to a global network of aerospace professionals.

Association of Women in Aviation Maintenance (AWAM)
website: www.awam.org

This nonprofit organization is dedicated to advancing women's professional growth and enrichment in aviation maintenance by providing opportunities for networking, sharing information, and education; fostering a sense of community; and increasing public awareness of women in the industry. Scholarships are offered to both male and female students.

Flight Safety Foundation
website: https://flightsafety.org

This global nonprofit organization provides a wide variety of resources for the aviation and aerospace community, including networking, publications, conferences, discounts on safety seminars, and much more. The foundation recently restructured its academic membership category to better serve students interested in aviation.

Geological and Petroleum Technician

What Does a Geological and Petroleum Technician Do?

Teens who enjoyed digging in the dirt or playing in the sandbox as kids may find their natural calling in this profession. Geological and petroleum technicians (GAPTs) search for valuable resources by analyzing samples of the earth's minerals and soil. They support engineers and scientists in a variety of duties. Many of their tasks are performed outdoors, and the open-air environment often attracts nature lovers to this line of work. "Geology is the study of how the earth changes, so I love getting outside and learning about and observing the earth's processes. It's a way for me to combine the recreational activities that I love with professional experiences," says Johnny MacLean, an associate professor of geology at Southern Utah University. "What better way to hang out outside and get paid for it."[18]

Erik Melchiorre, professor of geology at California State University, San Bernardino, agrees. In fact, he takes his students on outings to the Desert Studies Center in Zzyzx, California, where they conduct geological explorations.

"In geology and environmental sciences you really need to get out in the field, and that's why it is important to come to a site like this. Because if all you do is learn out of a book, you're not going to be ready for the workforce," he explains. "That's what I view my job as. I'm not training you to graduate; I'm training you to get a job and keep it."[19]

Tasks performed in the field include extracting and exploring natural resources like crude oil and minerals, as well as detecting natural gas. GAPTs use techniques such as borehole sampling, as well as electronic, sonic, and nuclear measurements, to determine the presence and size of oil, mineral, and gas deposits. In addition, these technicians may monitor borehole and well conditions. The results of their analyses may reveal a new site's potential for further exploration and development or may focus on monitoring the current and future productivity of an existing site.

After finishing their analysis, GAPTs write up their findings in reports that contain charts and graphs. GAPTs may also use another visual tool called a geographic information system, or GIS, to see what lies beneath the earth's surface. GIS systems are often used to produce three-dimensional images that help geologists who study earthquake faults, for example, or need other details. Oil and mining companies use GIS data to determine whether drilling or mining a site is safe, workable, and worth the financial investment. Another part of the technician's job is to evaluate existing mines, oil fields, and drilling equipment for safety and efficiency. If technicians see problems, they work with engineers to come up with solutions.

A Typical Workday

The daily work of GAPTs varies based on which organization they work for and whether they are inside a lab or working outdoors. In the field, they collect soil, minerals, rocks, and crude oil specimens from various depths. They work with specially designed drills and other devices to remove samples from bedrock. Bedrock is the hard layer of rock beneath looser rocks and soil. In some places, the bedrock is exposed, while in others it lies deep underground.

Going for the Gold

"As a geological technician at Dalradian Gold, I am part of the geology team that works on the drill core after it comes in from the exploration site. Working on a gold project is exciting . . . especially when you look at the recent gold find in Donegal of four solid gold rings dating back thousands of years. It shows how gold has played an important role in the lives of people on the island of Ireland for millennia, and I'm working on a project that carries on that tradition."

—Paddy Campbell, geological technician at Dalradian Gold in Northern Ireland

Quoted in Dalradian Gold, "Once in a Lifetime Opportunity," 2018. https://dalradianni.com.

These samples are transported to labs or offices, where GAPTs examine them using a microscope. GAPTs test the samples to figure out their chemical and physical properties. Canadian GAPT Steve Livie explains the process in detail:

> First, I wash the samples and put them on a drying rack for five to ten minutes. I then take these samples and put them on my examination tray and view them under the microscope. I move the rock pieces around with little tweezers. When [the samples are] under magnification, you can see them quite nicely. You have to have enough finger dexterity so you can pick up bits of rock. Translating the information that I see . . . through my microscope to what I see on the Pason screen, the EDR or Electronic Drilling Recorder, requires a bit of attention to detail.[20]

The Pason EDR system that Livie mentions is a device that enables oil rigs to share drilling data, reports, and real-time well information with office-based workers. The system can also provide internet access for well site users. Whether using an EDR or just a regular computer, GAPTs must document their conclusions in reports, maps, drawings, and pictures that show which locations offer the most promising resources.

Education and Training

GAPTs typically need an associate's degree or two years of post-secondary training in applied science or a science-related technology at a community or vocational college. If a two-year course specifically for geological studies is offered, that would be all the better. If possible, students should prepare while still in high school, advises Darryl Maddox, who has worked as both a geologist and teacher. Maddox says:

> Lots of math, physics, chemistry and computer science [are necessary], and if you can find such a thing, art classes on sketching and making realistic detailed drawings. . . . [Math is crucial] because without it you can't do the physics and chemistry; physics and chemistry [is needed] because at the heart of the earth is a hydro-mechanical system with biological influences and minor modifications. Computer science [is a must] because databases are getting larger, analytical equipment and most observational equipment such as remote sensors . . . are computer controlled.[21]

Remote sensors collect data in the form of images and provide specialized capabilities for manipulating, analyzing, and visualizing those images.

Aspiring GAPTs can benefit from an internship or on-the-job training program with an experienced geological technician. Here they will gain hands-on instruction on how to set up and use laboratory equipment and how to gather and organize samples. A variety of paid and unpaid internships are available from large employers such as Barrick Gold Corporation, ExxonMobil, and ConocoPhillips; government agencies such as the US Department of the Interior; and various small consulting firms and mining companies.

Skills and Personality

Would-be GAPTs should show an interest in working with math, science, and computers and possess an aptitude for numbers and statistics. Along with knowledge of chemistry, geography, and physics, GAPTs should like working outdoors and moving around from site to site. In addition, because of deadlines, they need to be able to work under pressure. They should also be team players. "Geology workers meet different people, so they have to get along with a lot of different personalities," says Joshua R. Feffer, owner and founder of Feffer Geological Consulting in Los Angeles. "They also should be able to think on their feet because issues come up all the time. They have to be problem solvers."[22]

Working Conditions

Working as a GAPT requires a spirit of adventure and a tolerance for changing weather conditions. These technicians spend a lot of time outdoors, often in the heat and the cold in remote locations. Even though some mines and drill sites are situated near well-populated areas, many are located in far-flung places, including offshore drill sites. Susan Flasha, a senior project geologist, sometimes takes her geology technicians to the Brucejack Mine, a high-grade underground gold mine located in northwestern British Columbia. Jokingly calling herself and her technicians "gold diggers," she describes the lengthy, multi-transit trek from Vancouver to the Canadian backcountry. "To get here, we took a two-hour plane ride from Vancouver, then hopped in a van to drive on a highway for five hours, and then boarded a helicopter to land here in Brucejack." Flasha adds that she and her team enjoy the work very much despite the logistical challenges. "I love that I'm doing something different every day."[23]

Besides at remote locations, laboratory specialists may work in their organization's offices and labs located in towns or cities, putting in a standard five-day workweek. Safety is an issue for GAPTs who work near drill sites and mines, and falls and accidents sometimes occur. At mining sites, rock slides and cave-ins are always possible, regardless of how careful the workers are. To protect themselves while out in the field, GAPTs observe strict safety rules and wear protective gear that includes safety glasses, hard hats, and steel-toe boots. They might also wear respirators if there is a chance of exposure to coal dust, for example.

Paid to Play in the Dirt

"Going to work every day seems more like play than work. I joke with friends that I get paid for playing in the dirt. I go to job sites collecting soil samples and sending them to a lab for identification. A key task is performing a sand cone test—measuring the dry density and moisture content in the soil after compaction to see how much water is present. This helps determine if an area is safe for building. I have to say that I really like my working conditions. Living in California means I often get to see the ocean while I work."

—Daniel Greene, geology field technician for Feffer Geological Consulting in Los Angeles

Daniel Greene, telephone interview with the author, September 26, 2019.

Employers and Pay

The median annual wage for GAPTs was $53,300 in 2018; ($105,000 for senior-level technicians), or $25.62 per hour according to a report from the Bureau of Labor Statistics (BLS). Technicians receive the highest compensation in Nevada, Texas, Louisiana, and California, where they can earn as much as $81,800, according to a 2019 post on the career website Recruiter.com. The specific industry sector in which GAPTs work also determines their salary. For example, those who work in oil and gas extraction earn $70,890 a year, according to the BLS, while those who work for an engineering services company earn about $45,200.

What Is the Future Outlook for GAPTs?

Employment of GAPTs is projected to grow by 14 percent through 2028, much more than the average for all occupations, according to the BLS. Demand for petroleum and natural gas, along with exploration of resources such as metals and minerals, is expected to increase demand for geological exploration and extraction in the future, says the BLS. Job opportunities will also stem from the need to replace workers who leave the occupation permanently because of retirement. The best job prospects will be for those candidates who have had hands-on training and possess solid technical and analytical skills.

Find Out More

American Association of Petroleum Geologists (AAPG)
website: www.aapg.org

As the world's premier professional association for oil explorers, the AAPG is about the science of petroleum geology. The AAPG, a nonprofit organization, provides publications, conferences, and educational opportunities to geoscientists and disseminates the most current geological information available to the general public. AAPG membership includes over eight thousand students.

Association of Environmental & Engineering Geologists (AEG)
website: www.aegweb.org

The AEG offers an extensive array of opportunities for students and educators with online resources, publications, meetings, and seminars. AEG chapter meetings enable students and educators to interact with practicing professionals and learn more about applied geology. The AEG also supports student chapters at more than two dozen universities.

EnvironmentalScience.org
website: www.environmentalscience.org

EnvironmentalScience.org is an organization that promotes environmental science education and careers. Its website offers information about different environmental careers, including GAPT.

Nevada Mining Association
website: www.nevadamining.org

This association promotes Nevada's mining industry. Its website provides information about different mining careers, including geological technician; information about mining; and interviews with people in related fields.

Biomedical Engineering Technician

What Does a Biomedical Engineering Technician Do?

Biomedical engineering technicians (BMETs) repair and maintain medical equipment used in hospitals, nursing homes, and doctors' offices. When a computed tomography (CT) scanner, magnetic resonance imaging (MRI) scanner, or other piece of important medical equipment breaks down, BMETs troubleshoot the problem and repair the equipment on the spot. Both CT and MRI scans are used to take images within a patient's body to detect a tumor, fracture, or other medical condition. MRIs use radio waves, and CT scans use X-rays. Some BMETs use screwdrivers and soldering irons to make physical adjustments to the equipment, while others update specialized computer software used to calibrate the devices. Calibration ensures the equipment is performing accurately.

Some technicians specialize in repairing a specific type of medical equipment, while others are trained to maintain a variety of complex medical devices. "Imaging equipment techs [those who repair MRIs and CT scanners] make more money than other repair technicians, but they need to be available on weekends, and they often work overtime because repairing this equipment is so crucial,"[24] explains Steven Rubino, a senior manager who hires and supervises the BMETs who work for Scripps Health, a group of hospitals in San Diego.

In addition to making important repairs by a deadline, technicians perform maintenance and replace outdated equipment. "BMETs contribute enormously to successful patient outcomes in healthcare by inspecting, repairing, calibrating and designing medical equipment that grows more advanced and vital all the time,"[25] says Mary Zieglar, a biomedical doctoral student at the University of California, Irvine.

BMETs use their skills to prevent mechanical and computer errors that could harm patients or lead doctors to make a wrong diagnosis. They also set up preventive maintenance programs to keep equipment running and prevent life-threatening breakdowns. To test and repair equipment, BMETs must be able to use devices ranging from hand tools and soldering irons to computers and multimeters. A soldering iron has a heated metal tip and an insulated handle and is used to fasten metal parts together. A multimeter is an electronic device that measures electrical voltage, current, and resistance. After completing the repairs or maintenance, BMETs must document what they have done and submit the information to various regulatory organizations. "Federal regulations, especially the Centers for Medicare and Medicaid (CMS), require that we document repair work,"[26] says Rubino.

A Typical Workday

Katie Lapel, a BMET at Scripps Memorial Hospital in La Jolla, California, is one of two technicians trained to maintain and repair anesthesia machines at the busy hospital. An anesthesia machine is a medical device that administers the gases that put patients to sleep during surgery so they will not feel any pain. Most surgeries begin early in the morning, which means that Lapel needs to be in the operating room (OR) beforehand to assist the medical staff. "It's hard to get up before 5 a.m. each day, but it's nice being the one that the OR can count on,"[27] she says. Before the surgeries begin, Lapel and her coworker check on the OR equipment to make sure everything is working well.

To do her job, Lapel must stay calm in emergencies and be able to handle seeing patients mid-surgery. She says:

> The first time that I walked into an open-heart surgery, it was a little intimidating. The trick is to not focus on the fact that someone is lying on the table with their heart exposed to the world. Simple, right? It's not. But you try your best. You need to focus on the problem at hand. You need to help the doctor with their problem so that you can get in and get out as quickly as possible.[28]

Away from the operating room, BMETs typically work on a variety of other medical devices. They will also check and calibrate ventilators, which are respirators, or breathing machines, that provide patients with oxygen when they are unable to breathe on their own. They also work on defibrillators, devices that restore a normal heartbeat by sending an electric pulse, or shock, to the heart. These are used to prevent or correct an arrhythmia, a heartbeat that is uneven, too slow, or too fast. Defibrillators can also restart a heart's beating if it suddenly stops. BMETs may also work on infant warmers, which maintain a baby's body temperature. Other common medical devices BMETs tend to are electrosurgical units, which are used to do surgical cutting or control bleeding.

Education and Training

BMETs generally require a minimum of an associate's degree in electronics or medical technology from a community or vocational college, with course work in biomedical equipment repair. However, some employers will train applicants who have equivalent military training or related work experience in electronics or computer technology. Earning a Biomedical Equipment Technician certification, which is offered through the Association for the Advancement of Medical Instrumentation, will enhance job prospects for biomedical engineering technology professionals.

High-school students can get a head start by taking advanced math and science classes. "Try your best to take calculus in high school," advises Natalie Kalos, a biomedical engineering graduate from Cornell University. "Try some of the AP courses if you can fit [them] in without sacrificing the core intro classes. Do this and you'll be much further ahead when you start your college courses, since you will already know a lot of fundamentals."[29]

Paid and unpaid internships are a great way for BMET students to learn on the job and in many cases to get paid for doing so. The best employers for internships include large medical device companies such as Stryker, Smith & Nephew, Fresenius Medical Care, various children's hospitals nationwide, the Mayo Clinic, and many other organizations that are eager to train future BMETs. To find out about opportunities, students should check out individual company websites as well as career websites such as Simply Hired.

Skills and Personality

Besides being detail oriented with a strong problem-solving ability, technicians should be able to read mechanical drawings and technical documentation. BMETs also need strong communication skills

Using Your Head and Your Hands

"It's a well-balanced career. You go from using your head to using your hands. You have to think to resolve a problem and then you use your hands and your work to actually create that solution. You get to work with a team: doctors, nurses, [and] your other technicians on projects, and then you also get to work as an individual where you can use your own ideas and your own hard work and then you actually see that manifest into a sense of satisfaction, a job well done. Like I took something that was broken and now it's fixed and it can be used for a patient and help make a doctor's job easier."

—Joseph Mollo, biomedical technician at Children's Hospital of Philadelphia

Joseph Mollo, "Biomedical Equipment Technology Program Alumni," YouTube video, July 20, 2015. www.youtube.com/watch?v=LPX8I6Ht2hl.

because they often work in a team environment that requires them to connect with their colleagues, supervisors, managers, and customers. "A great BMET should be able to communicate (orally and in writing) how they diagnosed any issue with the medical equipment, how they determined the repair options, and how the repair was completed," writes technology reporter Briana Shearer. They also need exceptional attention to detail and a precision mindset. "BMETs service . . . life-saving medical equipment!" Shearer says. "One misstep could result in serious or deadly implications for a patient. This means that they are required to adhere to strict safety regulations and restrictions while performing their work."[30] BMETs must also be committed to learning new skills and keeping up with rapidly changing biomedical engineering technology.

Working Conditions

BMETs work indoors in hospitals as well as in offices and laboratories of medical suppliers and companies that manage facilities throughout the United States. They usually work in shifts and wear uniforms, and some start very early in the morning. Perhaps most important of all, BMETs usually work under stressful conditions because of the life-or-death nature of their profession. For that reason, it is important to stay cool under pressure and enjoy working in a fast-paced environment. "To say that biomed is a high intensity job is an understatement," says Lapel. "Sometimes you have downtime when you can do paperwork and catch up; other times, not so much. You're usually running from the time that you get there in the morning to the time that you leave."[31]

In a hospital setting such as where Lapel works, BMETs must be comfortable working around patients because repairs sometimes take place while equipment is being used. When this is the case, BMETs must take great care to ensure that their work activities do not disturb patients. One potential downside to working close to patients is the possibility of catching a disease or getting an infection. Also, BMETs who work as contractors to medical device companies or urgent care clinics that operate across different states often have to travel—sometimes long distances—to perform needed repairs. While some technicians may view this travel as adventurous, others may get tired of being on the road so often.

Employers and Pay

According to the Bureau of Labor Statistics (BLS), the 2018 median salary for BMETs is $46,340. The highest-paid 10 percent earn more than $76,350 a year. In addition to working for hospitals, BMETs also work for medical device manufacturers as well as electronic equipment repair and maintenance companies that service medical equipment used by doctors, dentists, veterinarians, and other health care professionals. While some BMETs are trained to fix many types of equipment, others specialize and become proficient at repairing just one type of machine.

What Is the Future Outlook for BMETs?

According to the BLS, employment of BMETs is projected to grow by 7 percent through 2028, about as much as the average for all occupations. As people get older, especially baby boomers (those from 1946 to 1964), they will require more medical services, which will in turn require the services of BMETs and other medical professionals. "BMETs are rarely laid off or outsourced and enjoy excellent job security,"[32] explains Mary Zieglar.

Find Out More

American Society for Engineering Education (ASEE) Biomedical Engineering Division
website: https://sites.asee.org/bed

The biomedical division of the renowned ASEE provides a vital forum for those interested in biomedical engineering education by providing workshops, research paper sessions, and panel discussions of current topics in this profession. Students can browse the website to learn about job openings and other valuable information.

American Society of Biomechanics (ASB)
website: www.asbweb.org

The ASB has a membership of approximately 850 academic researchers, clinicians, scientists, students, and industry members working to solve basic and applied biomechanical problems. Students can watch free videos and learn about the biomechanical profession by reviewing the site's valuable free information.

Biomedical Engineering Society (BMES)
website: www.bmes.org

The BMES is a global organization of professionals devoted to developing and using engineering and technology to advance human health and well-being. Students can learn about job openings, review archived webinars, and obtain a wide variety of biomedical career information for free.

Institute of Biological Engineering (IBE)
website: www.ibe.org

The IBE is a professional organization that encourages inquiry and interest in biological engineering. Students can learn about job openings and access a wide variety of free resources on its site. The IBE also supports scholarships in education, research, and service.

Civil Engineering Technician

A Few Facts

Number of Jobs
About 73,800 as of 2018

Pay
About $52,580 per year, or $25.28 per hour

Educational Requirements
Associate's degree

Personal Qualities
Analytical, mathematically inclined

Work Settings
Indoors in an office or laboratory and outdoors on a job site

Future Job Outlook
Growth of 7 percent through 2028

What Does a Civil Engineering Technician Do?

Civil engineering technicians are involved in the construction of infrastructure such as roads, schools, telephone lines, sewage treatment plants, and power plants. Teens who are good at math and have an interest in how big things are built would likely make good civil engineering technicians. These professionals work under the guidance and direction of civil engineers, who lead construction projects to build and repair the structures that communities and governments need for everyday living. Technicians make a valuable contribution because they observe progress on a job site, collect data, and complete reports that document project activities. They also help plan, design, and build commercial, industrial, residential, and land development projects. Their duties include reading and reviewing blueprints for infrastructure projects, inspecting project sites, and evaluating contractors' work to ensure that projects meet design specifications as well as federal, state, and local code requirements.

Technicians also identify problems with design plans, find solutions to them, and document all project activity. Despite all the details involved in civil engineering, this profession can be a lot of fun. "Do you enjoy playing with Legos? Do you love making sand castles at the beach?" asks Mithil Haldankar, a technician from Dubai, United Arab Emirates. "Civil engineering is just that except that here you are building big permanent structures that are going to last a longer time than your Lego blocks or sandcastles!"[33] Because they are not licensed, civil engineering technicians cannot approve designs or supervise the overall project. Instead, they assist civil engineers who do have design and supervision authority—as well as the ultimate responsibility for the project's success.

A Typical Workday

Technicians work on a wide variety of projects, so each day is different. They are involved in new projects from the very start; one of their responsibilities is to review blueprints and plans. When a city, say, outgrows its airport and needs a larger one, technicians help get the process rolling by developing plans and estimating construction costs for the expansion. When an obsolete water treatment system no longer meets the needs of a community, technicians help engineers design and construct a newer system. When studies show need for a new road or highway, technicians assist engineers by surveying the land. Surveying involves measuring a property's distances, directions, angles, and elevations to determine the best way to build on it. This data helps create accurate maps and determine plot boundaries.

Self-employed civil engineering technician Paul Hayes appreciates the varied duties of his profession. "I work out of my home office, and no two days are the same. I really enjoy the challenge . . . the diversity," he says. Hayes also appreciates the universal appeal of the work, as well as its stability. "I would recommend a career in [civil engineering] technology to anyone, male or female. You're never going to have a problem getting a job."[34]

On the job site, a technician might need to take soil samples to test later in the laboratory. Another on-site activity may involve evaluating construction materials and ensuring that the project conforms to the required building codes. A building code is a set of laws enacted by state, county, and city governments to determine the required design and construction standards for new structures. For example, building codes determine how electrical, plumbing, and framing must be built. In yet another outdoor job setting, technicians may set up and monitor different instruments for traffic studies.

Education and Training

Although not always required, it is preferable for a civil engineering technician to hold an associate's degree in civil engineering technology. In addition, technicians must be skilled in math and physics, as well as reading maps, reviewing blueprints, studying design techniques, and using computer-aided design software, especially AutoCAD, Civil 3D, and PDS.

Some vocational schools, such as St. Clair College in Ontario, Canada, offer cooperative work-study programs in which students spend half of their time attending classes and the other half working at a civil engineering consulting firm or government agency. Students receive a solid foundation in core subjects that

At a job site, a civil engineering technician and engineer check progress on a project. These techs are involved in various stages of planning, design, and construction.

balance theoretical and practical knowledge, and then they get to put their skills to work on a real job site. Work-study programs also expose students to different types of civil engineering projects. These may include, for example, planning, designing, and building highways, bridges, utilities, tunnels, or other structures for commercial, industrial, residential, and land development projects. "I picked the [civil engineering] program because it has a wide variety of fields you can enter after graduation," says Jonathan Kerr, a civil engineering technology student at St. Clair College. "That way you can pick what you like and focus your career on that."[35]

Paid and unpaid internships are a great way to gain experience in the civil engineering field. Large companies who hire interns include Stantec, AECOM, Tetra Tech, American Bridge Company, Jacobs, and others.

Skills and Personality

Civil engineering technicians need to be thinkers and doers. Critical thinking is vital because technicians must be able to help their engineers identify and solve problems that arise in infrastructure projects. Technicians must also come up with innovative ideas that prevent agencies from wasting time, effort, and money. "Don't be afraid to think outside the box," recommends retired civil engineer technician Dan Duarte. "Engineers often tend to be robotic and afraid of new things. When I'd get called in to problem-solve, one of the most common reactions I'd hear to my ideas was, 'But we've never done that before!' To which I'd reply, 'There's a first time for everything.'"[36]

Decision-making is another important skill to possess. Engineers often face strict deadlines; technicians must often work under pressure, and it helps if they are good at quickly figuring out which information is most important for the task at hand and which plan of action will best keep the project on schedule. Math skills are also critical. Civil engineering technicians use math to analyze, design, and troubleshoot various elements of their work.

It also helps to be very observant. Civil engineering technicians may need to go to a job site and assess a project's potential. To effectively do so, they must know what to look for and what to report back to the engineer who is overseeing the project. In other words, they must see beyond what is obvious to most onlookers and have a keen eye for detail. Consider, for example, a bridge. "Looking at it doesn't seem like much," says civil engineering technology student Danielle Tighe, "but if you actually look at the details and you wonder what is supporting that weight, what is supporting all that concrete or the cars and trucks above . . . I really pay attention to all of that now."[37]

Working Conditions

Civil engineering technicians can usually be found in their office, but they also visit job sites to inspect field conditions and work that is under way. They also test the materials that contractors use for projects. Occasionally, to meet a project deadline, they may be required to work long hours, weekends, or holidays, and some may need to relocate. "It may be necessary for some . . . to change residence every few years as their work takes them from one major engineering site to another,"[38] says Aklank Jain, who works for L&T Construction in West Bengal, India.

Despite all the details and deadlines involved in civil engineering, technicians often get great satisfaction out of working on projects that make life easier for citizens, such as roads, bridges, or tunnels that get people to their destinations in a safer, smoother way. "[It's really important to] have fun," advises Duarte. "Even if the hours are long and there seems to be a lot of pressure sometimes, you must find a way to enjoy it, otherwise, go do something else instead. People who are passionate about their work produce the best results."[39]

Employers and Pay

According to a 2018 report by the Bureau of Labor Statistics (BLS), 47 percent of civil engineering technicians work for local or state governments, and 44 percent of technicians work for companies in the architectural or engineering industries. The remaining 9 percent work for educational institutions such as schools and colleges as well as for construction companies. Technicians make about $52,580 per year, or $25.28 per hour. Civil engineering technicians who work for local government such as a city or a county earn about $10,000 a year more than those who work for a state government, according to the website Chron.

Although technicians who work for government agencies may not get paid as much in salary as those who work for large consulting firms, the health care and retirement benefits they receive may make up for the difference in money, as Ron Brees, a civil engineering technician for California's Elsinore Valley Municipal Water District, explains. "There are many great things about working within the public sector, and the benefits are the best I have had available to me since my days in the Navy."[40] Among the benefits Brees receives are full medical, dental, and vision care; reimbursement for educational expenses; and a retirement plan.

What Is the Future Outlook for Civil Engineering Technicians?

Jobs for civil engineering technicians are expected to grow by 7 percent through 2028, according to the BLS. These skilled workers will help preserve, repair, upgrade, and enhance the country's infrastructure as it gets older. Bridges, roads, levees, airports, and dams will need to be rebuilt, maintained, and upgraded. Also, a growing population means that water systems must be kept in good shape in order to reduce or eliminate loss of drinkable water.

Find Out More

American Society of Civil Engineers (ASCE)

website: www.asce.org

Founded in 1852, the ASCE is the United States' oldest engineering society. Its website offers education and career information, as well as access to trade publications such as the *Civil Engineering* magazine, with articles about the most critical issues facing civil engineers today and in the future.

Earthquake Engineering Research Institute (EERI)
website: www.eeri.org

The EERI is a technical society of civil engineers, scientists, and other professionals devoted to reducing the risks associated with earthquakes. Its website offers information about student activities, public policy, current projects, news articles, and a link to the *Pulse* e-newsletter.

EngineerGirl
website: www.engineergirl.org

The EngineerGirl website is designed to bring public attention to the many opportunities that engineering represents for girls and women, since females remain underrepresented in the engineering field. The website is a valuable resource for all kinds of information about engineering careers, including civil engineering.

Ultimate Civil Engineering Directory
website: www.tenlinks.com/engineering/civil

This online directory is packed with information about civil engineering and related topics. It offers information about bridges, building codes, dams and reservoirs, tall buildings and structures, and many other resources.

Occupational Health and Safety Technician

A Few Facts

Number of Jobs
About 19,200

Pay
About $50,780 per year in 2018

Educational Requirements
Associate's degree

Personal Qualities
Detail oriented, good critical-thinking skills

Work Settings
Indoors in an office or on a factory floor and outdoors at a construction site

Future Job Outlook
Growth of 7 percent through 2028

What Does an Occupational Health and Safety Technician Do?

Figures from the US Department of Labor show that every day, an average of fourteen workers are killed on the job, and more than twenty-five hundred Americans sustain workplace injuries or illness severe enough to miss days from work. With lawsuits increasing due to unsafe working conditions, a position as an occupational health and safety technician (OHST) could be a fulfilling career choice for conscientious and detail-oriented teens. Technicians typically work for occupational health and safety specialists—who are often their direct supervisors—to collect data on and analyze many types of work environments and work procedures. They also help inspect workplaces to make sure that the offices, factories, laboratories, and construction sites are safe for all workers and visitors. In addition, they help conduct tests and measure hazards to prevent harm to workers, property, the environment, and the general public. These hazards can include fires, toxic chemical spills, security breaches, and

Keeping Everyone Safe, Every Day

"My goal is to make sure everyone goes home safely every day. We do CPR [cardiopulmonary resuscitation] classes and OSHA [Occupational Safety and Health Administration] training. We walk the job sites and do a checklist to make sure everything is being done correctly [including] specific training for the specific jobs that we have. . . . I think the biggest thing is [being] a good communicator, and not just talking but listening. You have to listen to employees because they have a lot of input on how to do these jobs well and how to do these jobs safe[ly]."

—Suzanne Richards, safety manager, Lineberger Construction in Lancaster, SC

Quoted in YouTube, "A Day in the Life of a Safety Worker," YouTube, October 24, 2017. www.youtube.com/watch?v=eU_mzaGFmhw.

other risks that could hurt workers and prevent the business from making or selling its products on time.

Employees have the right to a safe workplace. The Occupational Safety and Health Act of 1970 (OSH Act) was passed to prevent workers from being killed or harmed at work. The law requires employers to provide their employees with working conditions that are free of known dangers. "As an employer, you have the duty to strive for a risk-free/harm-free workplace," says Brad Ottley, a safety consultant at Innovative Thinking Pty Ltd, in Johannesburg, South Africa. "This means continually assessing the work environment for potential hazards, understanding the risks these hazards possess and taking the steps to eliminate [them] where possible, and where you can't, reduce the likelihood of them causing harm to your employees."[41] If companies do not take steps to keep their workers safe, they are accountable to a higher power—the federal government agency known as the Occupational Safety and Health Administration (OSHA), which diligently regulates workplace safety. Most states have their own agencies similar to OSHA (the state equivalents are often called "baby OSHAs") that are charged with enforcing the comparable state regulations. In many cases, state regulations may exceed those of the federal government in terms of extensive workplace safety rules. It is important for technicians to be familiar with those state and federal laws. "A desire to learn is important as there are quite a few government regulations that you will need to be familiar with,"[42] says Don Schmid, a safety consultant and former global construction safety and risk manager for the Ford Motor Company.

A Typical Workday

Every day is different for an OHST. A day can start with checking emails or other communication from the previous work shift to determine whether there are any occupational health and safety incidents to follow up on. Management may hold a daily meeting to review the day's activities and to follow up on issues from the previous day. This is important because a technician's job involves both making recommendations to management—the executives who run the company—and supporting their decisions. "You will be in a position to make some tough calls," says Schmid. "This is where your experience, education and knowledge of people and the business come in."[43]

Making these tough calls may involve reviewing and commenting on a safe work procedure developed by a work team. If that procedure is lacking in some way, the OHST needs to let management know about the flaw or shortcoming and recommend ways to fix it. A key task for OHSTs in the construction industry, for example, is to make sure that workers are using required protective gear, such as masks and hard hats. OHSTs also assist their supervisor in conducting planned inspections of the workplace to see whether safety procedures are being followed. Examining tools is also important, as technician Cesar Martinez, who works for Achen-Gardner Construction, explains: "We have to inspect our tools every day, because if we have an extension cord that's cut or wet and is not properly inspected, it could get into the electricity and become an electrical hazard. Using air-powered tools instead of electrical tools—that eliminates the hazard. That's part of the planning and the training that we do."[44]

Because his work involves checking in on construction sites, a big part of Martinez's job requires driving to different job sites. While he enjoys the travel, this part of his occupation has its challenges, especially on rainy days. "When it's wet, we're working in trenches and excavations . . . after a while, the soil gets loose, and could fall and give, and an excavation could collapse," he says. Sometimes conditions become hazardous, at which point work should be paused. "Even though we have a critical job to do, the best thing to do sometimes is just stop the work,"[45] he adds.

Despite all of the safety precautions, accidents do happen—at outdoor construction sites, indoors on factory floors, in laboratories, and even in offices. When they do, the OHST works with management and employees to find out what happened and why and to correct and resolve the problem. Schmid explains the typical procedure:

> If there is an employee injury, the supervisor generally starts an investigation. Based on the seriousness of the injury, you may get involved as a member of the team, or lead the team in [an] investigation [of] how the incident happened, and what did we learn to prevent it from happening again. . . . Your work in this area will be similar to a police detective, involving witness statements, photographs, controlling the scene, evidence collection, etc.[46]

On more routine days, an OHST may be requested to provide safety information for a facility manager's presentation to executives or for an article on the company's website. Employees may have complaints or questions regarding whether a work condition or job task is safe. The OHST will provide an answer based on government and company requirements and a review with the safety team.

Education and Training

OHSTs typically enter the profession through one of two paths: getting on-the-job training or pursuing postsecondary education,

An occupational health and safety technician checks pressure gauges on a factory floor. These techs help with workplace inspections and the testing of equipment—all with an eye toward reducing hazards to workers.

such as an associate's degree or certification. Both paths will lead them to study specific laws and inspection procedures and learn how to conduct tests and recognize hazards. The length of training varies with a person's previous experience, level of education desired, and industry of interest.

Some technicians enter the field through a combination of related work experience and training. They may volunteer to take on health and safety tasks at their company even if it is not part of their original job description to do so. For example, an employee who works in another area of the company may volunteer to complete annual workstation inspections, stepping up to do this extra work without extra pay. This experience could lead to a job promotion as an OSHT. While not required, technicians can earn professional certifications from the Board of

The Daily Duties of a Health and Safety Coordinator

"I help develop safety training courses [and] prepare training manuals. I am responsible for inspecting the safety procedures and practices of contractors who work on the mine site. I train people to operate all of our gas detection equipment. I use audiometric equipment to perform hearing tests, and I always look for new ways to perform greater mine safety. If a safety incident does occur, I help prepare a report. And then I respond immediately to any recommendations that come out of the report to make sure a similar incident never happens again."

—Steve Hippisley, health and safety coordinator

Quoted in Mining Industry of Canada Human Resources Council, "Health and Safety Coordinator," YouTube, May 5, 2016. www.youtube.com/watch?v=zyHPTaRmKug.

Certified Safety Professionals, a not-for-profit corporation that offers accredited credentialing for safety, health, and environmental practitioners.

To get a head start on their careers, high school students interested in becoming OHSTs should take courses in English, math, chemistry, biology, and physics. "STEM [science, technology, engineering, and math]-related course work is definitely preferred," advises Schmid. "Experience in learning how things work, developing your abilities to be 'mechanically inclined' . . . where you are using your hands and mind to build, assemble disassemble and use tools is extremely helpful."[47]

Skills and Personality

OHSTs must be able to use advanced technology because they often work with complex testing equipment. Communication skills are also important to possess, since technicians need to communicate safety instructions and concerns to employees and managers. They frequently prepare written reports and deliver safety training to other workers. Also, attention to detail is vital, since OHSTs need to understand and follow safety standards and complex government regulations. Physical stamina is also required because OHSTs have to stand for long periods.

Working Conditions

OHSTs work in a variety of settings, such as offices, factories, or outdoors at construction sites. Their job often involves considerable fieldwork and travel. They may be exposed to strenuous, dangerous, or stressful conditions. They use gloves to avoid skin injuries such as burns, bruises, and cuts. They also wear helmets to prevent head trauma such as concussions. They may also use respirators to protect their lungs at a construction site. These and other personal protective and safety equipment are worn to minimize the risk of illness and injury.

Employers and Pay

According to the Bureau of Labor Statistics (BLS), in 2018 the largest employers of OHSTs were big-name manufacturers such as the Ford Motor Company, followed by government agencies, construction firms, management, scientific and technical consulting firms, and hospitals. OHSTs' median annual wage was $50,780. The lowest-paid 10 percent earned less than $32,080, and the highest-paid 10 percent earned more than $84,400. However, if OHSTs are promoted to specialists—a likelihood if they have worked for a few years—they could earn a median annual wage of $73,020.

What Is the Future Outlook for OHSTs?

The BLS projects that employment of OHSTs will grow by 7 percent through 2028, about as much as the average for all occupations. Technicians will be needed in a wide variety of industries to ensure that employers comply with both existing and new regulations.

Find Out More

American Society of Safety Professionals (ASSP)
website: www.assp.org

The ASSP provides education, advocacy, standards development, and a professional community to advance careers and the occupational health and safety profession as a whole. Students can learn more about the profession as well as how to apply for scholarships and grants by checking out the website.

Board of Certified Safety Professionals (BCSP)
website: www.bcsp.org

The BCSP is a not-for-profit corporation recognized as a leader in high-quality, accredited credentialing for safety, health, and environmental practitioners. The BCSP establishes standards and certifies competency criteria in professional safety practice. Students interested in a career in safety may refer to the organization's guide *The Safety Profession: Do You Have What It Takes?*

National Health and Safety Council
website: www.nsc.org

This well-known group works to eliminate preventable deaths at work, in homes and communities, and on the road through leadership, research, education, and advocacy. Members can access thousands of safety resources, including online learning via webinars and audio recordings. They can also compete for awards and recognition.

World Safety Organization
website: https://worldsafety.org

The World Safety Organization offers a broad selection of accredited professional certifications for environmental and occupational safety and health professionals worldwide. Free student membership is available for any student in middle or high school or in a college undergraduate or graduate degree program.

Drafter

A Few Facts

Number of Jobs
About 199,900 as of 2018

Pay
About $55,550 per year, or $26.71 per hour

Educational Requirements
Minimum of associate's degree

Personal Qualities
Spatial visualization skills, attention to detail, mathematical ability

Work Settings
Indoors in offices; freelance drafters can work remotely

Future Job Outlook
Growth of 7 percent through 2026

What Does a Drafter Do?

Teens who liked to build things as kids, including playing with Lego blocks, may be interested in a career that involves drafting. Drafters use computer software to convert the designs of engineers and architects into technical drawings. Most workers specialize in architectural, aeronautical, civil, electrical, or mechanical drafting and use technical drawings to design everything from microchips to skyscrapers.

Many drafters are referred to as computer-aided design (CAD) operators. CAD software is used by architects, engineers, drafters, artists, and other professionals to create two-dimensional (2-D) drawings or three-dimensional (3-D) models. Drafters work with CAD so they can draw schematics that can be viewed, printed, or programmed directly into building information modeling (BIM) systems. These systems allow drafters, architects, construction managers, and engineers to create digital models of physical buildings and machines. Through 3-D rendering, BIM software allows designers and engineers to see how different elements in their projects work together. Because mastering these and other programs is vital for working as a drafter, students considering this career need to feel comfortable learning the latest software. "You really have to know your way around drafting, especially CAD," says architectural drafter Sherry Mack. "You need to be super comfortable with technology."[48]

A Typical Workday

While all drafters need to master CAD and other software systems, their day-to-day duties vary depending on their field of specialization. Aeronautical drafters prepare engineering drawings that show detailed plans and specifications used to make aircraft, missiles, and related parts. Architectural drafters, on the other hand, draw out buildings' structural features. These workers may specialize in a type of building, such as residential housing, and projects might involve building new homes; or they might specialize in constructing commercial structures, such as an office building or store. They may also specialize in certain materials, such as steel, wood, or reinforced concrete.

As they begin their workday, drafters may participate in a morning project meeting, in which they interact with coworkers and supervisors. Drafting work is collaborative, so their daily schedules involve conversations with team members who have different types of skills. Each person is generally assigned to work on a particular part of the design project. "A typical day for me varies; it depends on the stage we are in with the projects we are working on," explains Allan Pfannmuller, who works as an architectural drafter for a construction engineering consulting company in Canada. "Early in a project I work . . . to map out a project for the size and types of pipes we're using. . . . We might [also] be modeling and taking the model into the field."[49] Pfannmuller is referring to the scale models that architects use to help them do their work better. Architects use these models for many reasons: they are a form of 3-D sketching and help architects visualize how light will illuminate spaces. The models also help architects analyze the best ways to construct a house or office building.

While civil drafters also use models, they mostly focus on preparing topographical maps for projects such as highways, bridges, and dams. A topographic map is a detailed 2-D representation of natural and human-made features on the earth's surface. Engineers use these maps to plan a wide variety of building activities.

Another type of drafter specializes in electrical designs and prepares wiring diagrams. Construction workers refer to the diagrams to install and repair electrical equipment and wiring in power plants, electrical distribution systems, and residential and commercial buildings. This kind of drafting can be really interesting, according to electrical drafter Jillian Knox of JK Designs. "In electrical drafting, there are so many different things you are doing," she says. "It could be drawing wiring diagrams, or working with schematics or even layout drawings."[50] Last but not least, mechanical drafters prepare layouts that detail a wide variety of machinery, tools, and devices, including medical equipment. Their layouts indicate dimensions, fastening methods, and other requirements needed to assemble the machine. A fastener is a device that is used to mechanically join two or more objects together. There are many different types of construction fasteners, and these are typically made of steel, titanium, or aluminum.

A drafter's computer-aided design (CAD) drawings are an important part of the process of design and construction. Drafters often specialize in one area—for instance, in architectural or electrical or mechanical drawings.

Education and Training

Drafters typically need an associate of applied science in drafting or a related degree from a community college or technical school. Some drafters earn a certificate (the American Design Drafting Association offers these) or diploma. Drafting courses teach design fundamentals, sketching, and CAD software. It generally takes about two years of full-time school to earn an associate's degree; certificate and diploma programs may be completed in less time. Although not required, certification can give job seekers an advantage when interviewing for jobs. Certifications are offered for several specialties, including architectural, civil, and mechanical drafting.

High school students may begin preparing for this career by taking classes in mathematics, science, computer technology, design, computer graphics, and where available, drafting. Whatever classes they take, high school students should have a positive attitude about learning. "Take time to learn to love the process of learning," advises Cathleen Jones, a CAD designer, author, and educator with thirty-five years of design experience. "[Drafting] is an industry where you have to continually upgrade your knowledge and skills, and that information is out there. You [just] have to go look for it." Jones also urges drafting students to develop a sense of pride in their work and to take ownership of their projects. "Treat every drawing that you make like it has your name on the company letterhead," she says. Jones also emphasizes the importance of students thinking carefully about what they are designing and how that particular design will affect the overall project. "Think through the entire design process whether you are arranging fruit or designing a bridge. Ask yourself, 'how is this design going to be used?'"[51]

Skills and Personality

Career experts say that successful drafters need a blend of technical and managerial skills. Creativity is also important because drafters must be able to turn plans and ideas into technical drawings of buildings, tools, and systems. Spatial skills—or the ability to visualize 2-D and 3-D objects in one's mind— are vital as well. "Spatial perception is quite important. It's important to look at a 2-D drawing and visualize a 3-D object,"[52] explains Pfannmuller.

Along with spatial visualizing, drafters need solid math skills as well as an eye for details. Because drafters often work under tight deadlines, they must also be good at managing their time efficiently. Interpersonal skills come in handy, too. "While technical skills are what enable CAD technicians to draw up plans and work effectively on a project, soft skills are what determine how well these professionals communicate with clients, cooperate in a team, stay organized and use creativity,"[53] notes the Digital School Technical Design College.

Working Conditions

Most drafters work indoors, sometimes in a noisy environment. They may also need to share office space with coworkers. If they are employed by an engineering consulting company that works in the mining, oil and gas, or pulp and paper industries, their work will likely take them outdoors as well. "We have to go into industrial environments quite often to collect field notes or scan data that can be hazardous," explains Pfannmuller. "We need the proper training and personal protection equipment [such as] high-visibility vests, hard hats and safety glasses." The upside of such work is that some drafters may be eligible to earn a higher hourly rate should they need to be out in the field longer than the typical workday. "If we're in a bit of crunch to finish a project," notes Pfannmuller, "there is overtime [pay] available."[54]

Employers and Pay

Indeed, pay is among the benefits attracting people to this job. In 2018 drafters earned a median annual pay of $55,550, according to the Bureau of Labor Statistics (BLS). The lowest-paid 10 percent earned less than $35,170, and the highest-paid 10 percent earned more than $85,140. Drafters who specialize in electronics and electrical systems tend to earn about $5,000 a year more than other drafters. The largest employers of drafters are architectural and engineering companies, at 49 percent, followed by manufacturing companies at 25 percent and the construction industry at 10 percent. Some drafters are self-employed and work for architectural and engineering companies on a contract basis either remotely or in the office. This provides them with a wide variety of experience and diverse assignments. The downside is they must always be looking for their next assignment or contract.

What Is the Future Outlook for Drafters?

Demand for drafting jobs is expected to be about average in the coming years, with growth at about 7 percent through 2026, according to the BLS. The need for particular drafting specialties varies across the country because jobs depend on the requirements of local industries. For example, job prospects for mechanical drafters are best in manufacturing hubs, which the Industry Today website reports as being Wichita, Kansas; Fort Wayne, Indiana;

Battle Creek, Michigan; Toledo, Ohio; Portland, Oregon; Wausau, Wisconsin; Reading, Pennsylvania; Clarksville, Tennessee; Boise, Idaho; and Janesville, Wisconsin. While some drafters go on to become engineers or architects, many are satisfied to stay in their specialized field, as Pfannmuller can confirm: "It's a good career. You don't have to go on to become an engineer; the industry needs more technicians."[55]

Find Out More

American Design Drafting Association (ADDA)
website: www.adda.org

The ADDA is a nonprofit professional educational organization that serves the professional growth and advancement of individuals, students, instructors, and related organizations working in the professional design drafting/graphics profession. Students can browse free job listings and learn about certifications, schools, and more.

Association for Computer Aided Design in Architecture (ACADIA)
website: http://acadia.org

ACADIA is an international network of digital design researchers and professionals that offers the latest information on the use of CAD in architecture, planning, and building science, encouraging innovation in design creativity, sustainability, and education. Students can browse CAD designs and connect with designers for free. In 2019 scholarships cosponsored by Autodesk and ACADIA totaled $10,000.

Electrical Engineering Portal
website: https://electrical-engineering-portal.com

The Electrical Engineering Portal is a valuable resource for anyone interested in a career in electrical engineering or drafting. The website offers articles on electrical engineering, explanations of various theories, high-quality engineering literature, research papers, and even a collection of downloadable software.

EngineerGirl
website: www.engineergirl.org

The EngineerGirl website is designed to bring public attention to the many opportunities that the engineering and drafting professions offer to girls and women, since females remain underrepresented in the field. The website is a valuable resource for all kinds of information about careers in engineering and drafting, including civil engineering.

Robotics Technician

A Few Facts

Number of Jobs
About 14,000 as of 2018

Pay
About $57,790 per year, or $27.78 per hour

Educational Requirements
Associate's degree or postsecondary certificate

Personal Qualities
Analytic, mathematically and scientifically inclined

Work Settings
Indoors in an office or laboratory setting or on a factory floor

Future Job Outlook
Growth of 7 to 9 percent through 2028

What Does a Robotics Technician Do?

Teens who are passionate about how technology works—whether it is a smartphone or other electronic device—may find their niche as a robotics technician. Sometimes called electromechanical technicians, these skilled workers combine their knowledge of mechanical technology with the ability to understand electronic circuits. They operate, test, and maintain unmanned, automated, robotic, or electromechanical equipment such as an automotive robot that drives screws into parts. These robots also assemble, paint, and weld the parts together that eventually become a car, truck, or other vehicle. Other types of robots are used by online retailers like Amazon. In fact, the retailer's warehouses are stocked with palletizers, which are robotic arms with grippers that identify and grab totes from conveyor belts and stack them on pallets for shipping or stowing.

Another type of robotic arm, called the robo-stow, lifts pallets of merchandise such as toys, books, or electronic gadgets to different levels in fulfillment

Troubleshooting Matters

"One of the most important skills is troubleshooting. You have to be able to look at a machine and track down the problem from start to finish. One of the systems has robotic arms which require adjustments on a daily basis. I basically hook up a joystick controller for the robot and put the machine in manual so I can reposition this robot arm and do a variety of tasks."

—Jessica Amsden, robotics technician for E-One Moli Energy

Quoted in IWITTS Robotics, "Female Role Model Career Video," YouTube, September 28, 2015. www.youtube.com.

centers (where customers' orders are shipped) or places them on drive units to be carried to their next destination. These robots—along with many others—all need to be programmed and maintained by robotics technicians. These technicians also read blueprints, schematics, and diagrams to determine how to assemble a part, machine, or piece of equipment. In addition, they analyze and record test results and prepare written documentation to describe the tests they performed and what the test results mean.

There are two kinds of robotics technicians. One type works with engineers and designers to assemble robots and test them. These technicians help develop the computer programs that control the robot and direct it to do tasks. These technicians understand computers, electronic systems, sensors, and the inner workings of robots and automation control systems. Other robotics technicians work with robots that are used in industrial manufacturing. They are responsible for maintaining and troubleshooting a robot's electrical and mechanical systems. Ensuring that a robot is functioning efficiently is important in order to keep the manufacturing floor making products. As a result, industrial robotics is poised to be a growing field. "There's a huge demand for qualified technicians who can program the robots and set them up to manufacture products,"[56] says Dorian McIntire, an instructor at Tri-County Technical College in South Carolina.

A Typical Workday

Robotics technicians often divide their workday between a manufacturing floor or lab and an office. Their floor or lab time may be spent working on small mechanical parts that are components of a larger robot they are helping build. Technicians also repair and maintain robots, assemble and test them, and program them to perform automated tasks. Office time may be spent reviewing and approving cost estimates and design calculations, working on plans, and writing reports.

Camden West of Fredericktown, Ohio, works for an automotive components manufacturer. He sets up robots to perform automated tasks such as trimming or polishing molds for car parts, like fenders and bumpers. "There are different moves you can program a robot to make. We enter information through a teach pendant, an external device that controls the robot," he explains. "Instead of teaching through the computer, it's on the robot itself." When something goes wrong, West figures out what the problem is and fixes it. "Most robots will sound an alarm and identify what that alarm means," he says. "For example, it might tell you one of the circuit boards is bad. It will give you the exact description of what's wrong and how to fix it. Sometimes that's as easy as going into maintenance mode and resetting the memory." West keeps his toolbox on the manufacturing factory floor in case he needs to make a repair. "I need to keep the robots and other equipment running at peak performance,"[57] he says.

Jessica Amsden is a robotics technician for E-One Moli Energy, a company that makes lithium ion batteries, the kind that recharge and have a longer life. Because of the delicate chemistry involved in making these batteries, certain parts of the manufacturing process must take place in a dry room, which has a humidity or moisture level of 1 percent or less. Too much moisture can harm the production of the batteries, while even a small intrusion of dust can have devastating consequences, such as causing a fire. For that reason, Amsden has to dress in protective clothing so she will not contaminate the room. Because lithium ion batteries are used in so many products, the company needs to fill its orders quickly and accurately. For that reason, the factory must operate at peak efficiency around the clock, as Amsden explains:

> We run 24/7, so a breakdown can easily occur from wear and tear and operator interference. When there's a breakdown, I discuss with the operator what the problem is, and I will go in and adjust sensors. Mechanical springs can become weak. Just moving parts can eventually hit each other. Anything [can go wrong] from errors or glitches in the program, which runs the actual assembly line.[58]

Education and Training

Most technician jobs require at least an associate's degree in robotic technology or a related major. "Some companies will even accept candidates with simply a high school diploma if they have two years or more of experience with robotics," writes Siobhan Treacy on the career website Engineering360. "There are also some companies that accept applicants with only a high school degree and then foster their training by placing them in a two-year training program."[59]

Students who are interested in robotics training have a number of options, ranging from self-paced online courses that take about a year to complete to two-year community college programs that combine online and classroom instruction along with work-study programs. Some of the most comprehensive two-year robotics programs are available at Oakland Community College in Auburn Hills, Michigan; Butler Community College in Pittsburgh, Pennsylvania; and St. Clair College in Ontario, Canada. "[We offer] . . . a very hands-on program . . . for work in industry," explains Joe Aarssen, robotics program coordinator at St. Clair College. "Students learn how to configure, set up, trouble-shoot, and find out what's going on with the robots. They learn how to take them from square one and configure

A robotics technician tests the function of a robotic arm used by a factory. These techs operate, test, and maintain robotic equipment.

them to any type of application. Then they spend a couple of different classes programming them."[60] After completing a program approved by the Accreditation Board for Engineering and Technology and gaining a few years of work experience, robotics technicians may pursue professional certification through the National Institute for Certification in Engineering Technologies, which requires applicants to pass a written exam, provide supervisor references, and complete a designated amount of in-school and on-the-job training.

Skills and Personality

Because robotics technicians make very precise, accurate measurements, they should be detail oriented. Manual dexterity is important, too, because technicians use hand tools and soldering irons on small circuitry and electronic parts to create detailed

Robots Are the Future

"For an individual to be successful, you should be a self-starter. . . . You're never just sitting somewhere. You're kind of always doing something. There are a lot of opportunities in the robotics industry. Robots are the way of the future. Everything breaks, especially robots. There's tons of room for new young individuals who want to do this. It is very lucrative to be in this industry."

—Johnny Node, robotics technician

Quoted in Express Employment Professionals, "Trending Career Tracks for Associate Degrees," YouTube, September 18, 2017. www.youtube.com/watch?v=15WNcurwBAU.

electronic components by hand. In addition to their technical talents, technicians also need people skills because they must take instruction well and offer advice when required. They also need to coordinate their work with coworkers. "Communication is big no matter what you're doing," says West. "Also, pretty much everything you deal with has some sort of scale or dimension, so you need to know how to read blueprints and recognize where robots are being used in the process."[61]

Working Conditions

Working as a robotics technician is often a one-person operation. When technicians are not working alone, they are often working in teams of two. Most technicians work a standard workweek (forty hours), though some might be on call or on staff in a factory, in case a robot breaks down. This is especially common if they work for a company that uses robotics twenty-four hours a day, seven days a week. Some travel may be required if a technician is employed by a robotics manufacturer, and many consider this to be a job perk. "You get to see and do a whole lot of things," says West. "I once went to Japan for a couple days to see the robots we had coming. You get to learn and work with new technology all the time."[62]

Employers and Pay

The salary for these skilled technicians varies widely, depending on location and organization. Compensation ranges from $40,000 to $60,000 depending on education and experience, according to the career website Recruiter.com. Robotics technicians are paid the highest in Alaska, where they can receive salaries of around $86,730. Still, the midwestern and southern parts of the United States offer the most opportunities in robotics because this is where the auto industry, which heavily uses robotics, is based. Michigan accounted for the highest employment level, followed by Ohio and Indiana. "Other significant users include electronics, rubber and plastics industries,"[63] writes technology reporter Rachel Layne.

What Is the Future Outlook for Robotics Technicians?

Employment for robotics technicians is projected to grow by 7 to 9 percent through 2028, according to the Bureau of Labor Statistics. Increased reliance on technology is projected to drive demand, as Mandy Orzechowski, robotics instructor at Tri-County Technical College in South Carolina, explains:

> Employers are looking for people who have the ability to grow . . . who are adaptable because the industry is continuing to change and evolve rapidly, and they have to change and evolve with it. You could be the person who gets that broken robot and figures out what went wrong with it. You can figure out how existing robotics could be made better, how they could be improved, how they could be made cheaper, how they could be made more robust. People who possess these technical and problem-solving skills . . . are going to be sought after. . . . You're going to be able to negotiate what you want.[64]

Find Out More

Accreditation Board for Engineering and Technology (ABET)
website: www.abet.org

ABET is a nonprofit, nongovernmental organization focusing on what engineering and technology students experience and learn. ABET's events, workshops, webinars, and accreditation-related materials are valuable professional development resources. Students interested in learning about robotics technician jobs can find out which schools and colleges would suit them best.

Association of Technology, Management, and Applied Engineering (ATMAE)
website: www.atmae.org

With students and professional members from more than five hundred companies, community colleges, and universities throughout the United States, ATMAE offers peer-to-peer networking, education, and professional development opportunities for career success. Students can access the website's career center, which lists job openings and offers other free information.

IEEE Robotics and Information Society
website: www.ieee-ras.org

The Institute of Electrical and Electronics Engineers (IEEE) is the world's largest professional association providing access to the industry's most essential technical information, networking opportunities, career development tools, and many other benefits. Students can learn about job listings and find a variety of other free resources on the organization's website.

Institute of Industrial and Systems Engineers (IISE)
website: https://www.iise.org

The IISE is the global association of productivity and efficiency professionals specializing in industrial engineering, including robotics and electromechanical work. The website offers a number of free resources, including job listings and other career information.

Source Notes

Great Careers at Half the Cost and Time

1. Tiffni Deeb, "The CIO Minute: Why an Associate's Degree Matters," EDUCAUSE Review, September 23, 2019. https://er.educause.edu.
2. Chris A. Pipesh, email interview with the author, September 30, 2019.
3. Casey Wutzke, email interview with the author, September 20, 2019.
4. Don Schmid, email interview with the author, October 16, 2019.

Environmental Engineering Technician

5. Quoted in Quora, "Is Environmental Engineering a Good Career Choice?," January 8, 2016. www.quora.com.
6. Kelly S. Meier, "Definition of Environmental Service Hospital Job," Chron, June 27, 2018. www.chron.com.
7. Dawn Rosenberg McKay, "A Day in the Life of an Environmental Technician," Balance Careers, June 25, 2019. www.thebalancecareers.com.
8. OwlGuru, "Being an Environmental Technician: What You Really Do," 2019. www.owlguru.com.
9. Joe Proulx, "The Best Engineering Jobs in the US," October 2018, *U.S. News & World Report*. https://money.usnews.com.

Aerospace Engineering and Operations Technician

10. MIAT College of Technology, "The Growth of the Airline Industry: An Aviation Mechanics Guide," June 26, 2018. www.miat.edu.
11. Your Free Career Test, "What Does an Aerospace Engineer Do?," 2019. www.yourfreecareertest.com.

12. Quoted in James Wynbrandt, "How to Become a Repair and Test Technician," *Flying*, May 7, 2018. www.flyingmag.com.
13. Elvis Michael, "How to Become an Aerospace Engineering Technician," Chron, 2017. www.chron.com.
14. Bureau of Labor Statistics, "Aerospace Engineering and Operations Technicians," 2018. www.bls.gov.
15. Wutzke, interview.
16. Pipesh, interview.
17. Pipesh, interview.

Geological and Petroleum Technician

18. Johnny MacLean, "Major Decisions: Geology," YouTube, August 25, 2015. https://www.youtube.com/watch?v=xHY72JSHrKY.
19. Erik Melchiorre, "Geology Students Gain Work Experience," YouTube, February 21, 2019. https://www.youtube.com/watch?v=TeM1sw_NPA8&t=81s.
20. Quoted in WorkBC's Career Trek, "Geological Technician," YouTube, April 28, 2016. https://www.youtube.com/watch?v=ww_C4j3wVEQ.
21. Quoted in Quora, "What Subjects Are Needed in High School to Become a Geologist in the Future?," September 17, 2017. www.quora.com.
22. Joshua R. Feffer, telephone interview with the author, September 26, 2019.
23. Susan Flasha, "Living the Mining Dream," YouTube, January 28, 2015. https://www.youtube.com/watch?v=kE9ZltAAj4E.

Biomedical Engineering Technician

24. Steven Rubino, telephone interview with the author, October 1, 2019.
25. Mary Zieglar, "What Does a Biomedical Equipment Technician Do?," Inner Body, December 13, 2018. www.innerbody.com.
26. Rubino, interview.
27. Katie Lapel, email interview with the author, October 4, 2019.
28. Lapel, interview.
29. Quoted in Quora, "What Classes Should I Take in High School if I Want to Be a Biomedical Engineer?," July 24, 2016. www.quora.com.

30. Briana Shearer, "Four Characteristics of a Great Biomedical Technician," SPBS Clinical Equipment Service, July 11, 2017. www.spbs.com.
31. Lapel, interview.
32. Zieglar, "What Does a Biomedical Equipment Technician Do?"

Civil Engineering Technician

33. Quoted in Quora," Is Civil Engineering Fun?," May 27, 2017. www.quora.com.
34. Paul Hayes, "Civil Engineering Technologist," October 11, 2016. https://www.youtube.com/watch?v=UAzm4_KfQds.
35. Jonathan Kerr, "Civil Engineering Technology," YouTube, January 30, 2015. https://www.youtube.com/watch?v=QZ9mV1a TAYU.
36. Quoted in Quora, "What Does Every Civil Engineer Need to Know?," August 23, 2019. www.quora.com.
37. Danielle Tighe, "Civil Engineering Technology," YouTube, January 30, 2015. https://www.youtube.com/watch?v=QZ9mV1a TAYU.com.
38. Quoted in Quora, "What Does a Civil Engineer Do?," March 13, 2013. https://www.quora.com/profile/Aklank-Jain-1.
39. Quoted in Quora, "What Does Every Civil Engineer Need to Know?," August 23, 2019. www.quora.com.
40. Ron Brees, email interview with the author, October 2, 2019.

Occupational Health and Safety Technician

41. Quoted in Quora, "How Can Workplace Safety Be Ensured by the Employers?," October 9, 2019. www.quora.com.
42. Schmid, interview.
43. Schmid, interview.
44. Quoted in I Build America, "A Day in the Life: The Safety Manager," YouTube, January 26, 2016. www.youtube.com/watch?v=xHYOFjobc88.
45. Quoted in I Build America, "A Day in the Life."
46. Schmid, interview.
47. Schmid, interview.

Drafter

48. Quoted in California Community Colleges, "A Day in the Life of an Architectural Drafter," December 15, 2018. www.you tube.com/watch?v=edOxBPzwdqA&list=.

49. Quoted in "Drafting Technician (Episode 133)," YouTube, July 13, 2018. https://www.youtube.com/watch?v=TqqHy E3AZns.

50. Quoted in California Community Colleges, "A Day in the Life of an Electrical Drafter," YouTube, December 18, 2018. www .youtube.com/watch?v=fLt4JMlsXzo.

51. Quoted in AutoCAD, "7 Rules for Success for Designers and Drafters," YouTube, June 29, 2017. www.youtube.com /watch?v=uKHrJLBbJAs.

52. Quoted in WorkBC's Career Trek, "Drafting Technician."

53. Digital School Technical Design College, "3 Essential Skills You Need to Become a Successful CAD Technician," 2019. www.digitalschool.ca.

54. Quoted in WorkBC's Career Trek, "Drafting Technician."

55. Quoted in WorkBC's Career Trek, "Drafting Technician."

Robotics Technician

56. Dorian McIntyre, "Robotics Careers," YouTube, August 3, 2017. https://www.youtube.com/watch?v=xVVwYmRxaMgSciTrends.

57. Quoted in Elka Torpey, "Robotics Technician," Bureau of Labor Statistics, 2018. www.bls.gov.

58. Quoted in IWITTS, "Robotics—Female Role Model Career Video," YouTube, September 28, 2015. www.youtube.com /watch?v=jdzsJxXqWFU.

59. Siobhan Treacy, "How to Become a Robotics Technician," Engineering360, April 27, 2017. https://insights.globalspec.com.

60. Joe Aarssen, "Electromechanical Engineering Technician–Robotics," May 16, 2016. https://www.youtube.com/watch ?v=w-O2uHH7HVQYouTube.

61. Quoted in Torpey, "Robotics Technician."

62. Quoted in Torpey, "Robotics Technician."

63. Rachel Layne, "Which Industries Use the Most Robots?," CBS News, August 17, 2017. www.cbsnews.com.

64. Quoted in SciTrends, "Robotics Careers," YouTube, August 3, 2017. www.youtube.com/watch?v=xVVwYmRxaMg.

Interview with a Civil Engineering Technician

Ron Brees is a civil engineering technician who manages various projects for the Elsinore Valley Municipal Water District (EVMWD) in Lake Elsinore, California. Brees especially enjoys working with hands-on computer technology. He uses it to create visually detailed maps and other informational tools that help his team assist property owners and other customers with constructing a brand-new house or adding a room to their existing one. He answered questions about his career via email and a telephone interview with the author in September 2019.

Q: How did you get started as a civil engineering technician?
A: My career definitely did not take a linear path. I joined the navy at age 18, owned my own business after leaving the military a few years later, and ended up as a file clerk for a petrochemical company. While there, I taught myself AutoCad. By learning this program and showing an aptitude for digitizing aerial pictures, I was eventually promoted to a designer position. During the next few years, I worked as a land development designer for various companies. Then after a layoff in 2008 due to the recession, I was able to get a temporary position at American States Water Company. This is a private company that contracts with the government to deliver water to residents. When that position was over, a recruiter called me for a temporary position at Elsinore Valley Municipal Water District. I eventually got hired full time, and my position has evolved over the years as I have taken on more responsibility. I have now worked as an engineering tech for nine years.

Q: Can you describe your typical workday?
A: No day is typical, but what I do the most is check on projects, call designers, contractors, construction managers, and various

city engineers to work out different issues or gather information for use on a particular project. I write a ton of emails, memos, and create quite a few Excel spreadsheets for tracking information. [Excel is software used for storing, analyzing, and organizing data.] As part of this position I also check the credentials of outside contractors to make sure they are qualified to work for EVMWD.

Q: How has your position at EVMWD changed over the years?
A: I began my work at EVMWD by putting together basic exhibits, small designs, helping to locate plans and information, and maintaining the record drawings. . . . By "doing basic exhibits," I mean that I take what the engineer is thinking about the project and I make a pretty drawing out of it on the computer [using geographic information system, or GIS, software]. . . . Utilities must know where their pipes, valves, pumps, meters, and other facilities are located. They also need to know the location and water usage patterns of their customers. And they need to know where their crews are working and what facilities need maintenance. GIS helps with all of this.

Q: What courses in high school or college were most helpful to you in becoming an engineering technician?
A: I would say that the best teacher for me has been experience. I have not had a course or class that has shown me anything more than what I have learned through trial and error at being in my position. With that said, I would advise young people who want to work as an engineering tech to attend two-year programs at vocational or community colleges that offer the appropriate coursework. This includes science and math courses, such as chemistry, physics, geometry, and trigonometry. Of course, students should feel comfortable working on a computer, which most of them do now. Then, at a community or vocational college, they can also take design classes such as AutoCad and GIS.

Q: What do you like most about your job?

A: The best thing about my job is the fact that I can leave at the end of the day knowing I did the best I could in the best interest of the public. I really enjoy the interactions and figuring out solutions to issues that have not come up before. I get great satisfaction from knowing that what I do is serving the public and improving the lives of our residents. Getting water to people who need it is really important, and my work makes that happen. The work I do for our government agency helps people with the basic need for water that they use every day to live.

Q: What do you like least about your job?

A: The paperwork. By that I mean the forms that are required to be filled out for nearly everything we do. I understand the need but there are more times than not I would rather be working on a problem than filling in a form.

Q: What personal qualities do you find most valuable for this type of work?

A: The best type of personal qualities for being in this position would be a positive attitude, good work ethic, and willingness to listen.

Q: What is the best advice you can give to young people who are entering the working world for the first time?

A: I tell my student interns . . . to never turn down an opportunity because the job seems beneath you. You can always learn something. Then with the experience you get from that opportunity, you can move up to a better position. Experience is always key.

Other Jobs in Engineering

Aerospace mechanic
Aircraft mechanic
Aircraft technician
Airframe and power plant
  mechanic
Airplane mechanic
Airplane technician
Air quality specialist
Architecture and engineering
  drafting technician
Aviation technician
Biofuels processing technician
Building information modeling
  technician
Building services technician
CAD designer
Cartographer
Construction and building
  inspector
CT technician

Design technician
Drafting and design technician
Electronic engineering
  technician
Energy conservation technician
Engineering technician
Environmental science and
  protection technician
Fire inspector
Health and safety technician
Industrial designer
Mechanical engineering
  technician
Medical imaging technician
MRI technician
Petroleum technician
Radiology technician
Surveying and mapping
  technician
Ultrasound technician

Editor's note: The online *Occupational Outlook Handbook* of the US Department of Labor's Bureau of Labor Statistics is an excellent source of information on jobs in hundreds of career fields, including many of those listed here. The *Occupational Outlook Handbook* may be accessed online at www.bls.gov/ooh.

Index